TORRO, THE SILLY PARROT

by Virginia Loving Pope

Illustrated by Terri Kelleher

D1421985

© 2014 Virginia Loving Pope. All rights reserved.

No part of this book may be reproduced, stored in a retrieval system, or
transmitted by any means without the written permission of the author.

AuthorHouse™
1663 Liberty Drive
Bloomington, IN 47403
www.authorhouse.com
Phone: 833-262-8899

Because of the dynamic nature of the Internet, any web addresses or links contained in this book may have changed
since publication and may no longer be valid. The views expressed in this work are solely those of the author and do
not necessarily reflect the views of the publisher, and the publisher hereby disclaims any responsibility for them.

Any people depicted in stock imagery provided by Getty Images are models,
and such images are being used for illustrative purposes only.
Certain stock imagery © Getty Images.

This book is printed on acid-free paper.

ISBN: 978-1-4969-5988-1 (sc)
ISBN: 978-1-6655-6772-5 (hc)
ISBN: 978-1-4969-5989-8 (e)

Print information available on the last page.

Published by AuthorHouse 08/10/2022

authorHOUSE®

I first met my mommy in a faraway place. I was in a marketplace for sale for $8.00. Nobody wanted me. I was in a small wire cage and half of my feathers were missing. I WAS SO SAD!! All of a sudden I saw a beautiful girl paying the man $8.00 and she took me lovingly home to a hotel where she was staying with a girlfriend. They gave me fresh water and fruit.

I wanted to make her happy, so when they giggled in the night,I giggled too!! When they brushed their teeth in the morning,I imitated them with gargling sounds. THEY THOUGHT I WAS FUNNY!!

I heard them say, "Let's take him for a walk on the beach!" YEAH!! LET ME OUT OF THE CAGE!! I was so happy. MY LIFE HAD BEGUN!! When they went sight-seeing, I sat on the bus driver's shoulder. I also got to ride on the handle bars. I learned laughing, sneezing, coughing, and two poems from the bus driver that I have never forgotten. I AM SO HAPPY!!

My mommy took me home when her vacation was over. I was put into a special shelter for animals coming into the country for six weeks. I sat on the veterinarian's shoulder and drank out of his cup of coffee. I knew I had to be good so I could be with my mommy again. When she visited, I heard him ask if he could buy me, but she said, "NO!" and took me home.

She had a large cage and let me free during the day. I would play tricks on her to make her laugh. When I heard the key in the door, I would flatten my wings and slide behind the door.

She would be calling me, and finally when in tears and would open the door, I would fall out and say, "HI!"

Hi Mommy!

My mommy fed me scrambled eggs, my favorite, corn, fruit,seeds, and coffee with milk every morning. I could hardly wait!! We put make-up on together and I had my own set of brushes. It was my favorite time of day!! I also took showers and sang.

My mommy had a maid named Ella and she would come once a week. She wore the craziest shoes and boots. They had laces up and down, and lots of buckles. I would fly onto her leg and ride on the vacuum. We would sing and dance with the radio. The handy man would come up and I would play in his toolbox. He thought I was funny. I AM HAVING SO MUCH FUN!!

Sometimes my mommy would take me outside and she would walk down the street with me on her shoulder, under her long hair. We would go to banks and stores. I would sing and whistle and people thought it was her. HA, HA!! My mommy would laugh. We were having FUN!!

When it was time to have my nails and beak clipped, my mommy would take me to the animal hospital. I HAD FUN THERE!! I would tease the sick cats and dogs by barking and meowing. I would flirt with the nurses there and whistle at them.

When it came time to clip my beak, they took out big gloves and I would scream so loud that everyone could hear me down the hallway.

At times, I did not want to go to sleep early, and hide under her huge bed. Mommy would let me stay there all night and I would wake her up in the morning by giggling in her ear.

Mommy enjoyed it as much as I did!!

My mommy would buy me battery operated toys and I loved to chase them on her pretty table. Her friends would come by to watch my show. I LOVE PERFORMING!! Mommy once gave me a sweet sixteen birthday party, and I even got more toys. I knocked them off the table and laughed, and laughed.

My favorite time of day is watching tv in bed with my mommy at night. WE ARE SO SNUGGLY!!

Once, I was playing with the latch of the shutter on our house. I fell out of the window and landed on the roof of the house across the street.

My mommy called the Fire Department, and when they climbed up to get me on their ladder, I flew down and landed on my mommy's head and said, "HI!!" Everyone laughed.

I also went to a baseball game and sat on my mommy's shoulder and screamed louder than anyone else. My picture was on the front of every sports paper across the country.
THE FIRST PARROT TO ATTEND A BASEBALL GAME!! HA, HA!!

One day I was playing in the trees in my mommy's back yard.

All of a sudden two boys climbed the tree and took me into their house. They thought I was lost! I just sat there so sad while the boys talked silly to me. They gave me food and water but I did not want it. I thought about my mommy and how sad she must be. I could just imagine how I hurt her. I longed for her loving touch, her laugh, her smile, the fun we had together. I would never see my mommy again. MY WONDERFUL LIFE WAS OVER!!

It seemed like a long, long time and all of a sudden there was a loud knock on the boy's door. IT WAS MY MOMMY!! She had come to rescue me. A neighbor saw what happened and told her. She was crying and told the boys I belong to her. I flew onto her shoulder and snuggled under her golden hair. I never felt so safe and happy. She kissed and kissed me!!

Tears were running down her face. We laughed and we cried as we skipped happily back home. I WILL NEVER WANDER OFF AGAIN!!

'Torro, the Silly Parrot' is a delightful, whimsical story about the unique bonding and love between a famous parrot and his fashion model "Mommy."

You will travel with them from Colombia, South America, to the United States and relish in their day to day activities.

Torro's funny antics and his love of life, and especially, for his precious mommy will touch your heart.

The colourful, beautiful illustrations will mesmerize both children and adults alike. It is a touching, moving lesson on love, between a silly but intelligent parrot, and his devoted, caring mother.

This is one of the best children's books I have read in a long time. My 5 year old granddaughter is mesmerized by it, and it has become her favorite story, as it will for all young children and the young at heart.

-Helena C. Farrell, Author and Playwright

CPSIA information can be obtained
at www.ICGtesting.com
Printed in the USA
LVHW071743150323
PP17688900002B/2

9 781496 959881